Tragedy in the Arugula Aisle

Poetry

Charles W. Brice

ARROYO SECO PRESS

Logo by Morgan G Robles

Editor: LeAnne Hunt

Arroyo Seco Press

www.arroyosecopress.org

Cover art: Jim Hutt

ISBN: 979-8-9918724-0-9

For David Kirby
and in loving memory
of Steve Cawte

Poems

I		1
Tragedy in the Arugula Aisle		2
Toads in Bermuda		3
The Big Questions		5
St. Charles Borromeo		6
Laundry		8
Mother Wort		9
Lunch with CNN		10
First Subway Ride, 1974		12
Dufusyokelsplat		13
My First Rodeo		14
I'm Not Writing a Poem		16
Ice Jam		17
Hypocrititis		18
Eraser Poem		19
Dasein's Destiny		20
Bring 'Em Young		22
Blawnox		24
Assault and Battery		25

II		27
Standing Against Wyoming Wind		28
Rattle Bag		30
Love Bumps		32
Love		34
All In a Dream		35
Ice shelf		36
Getting It Right		37
The Hearty Roar of Autumn		38
Let It Be		39
Immortality		40
The Fortress		41
Last Words		42
Shadows on Our Bedroom Floor		44
Grace		45
Stinky		46

III   47

Boiled Dinners..48
Dodgeball...50
The Green Chair 51
Grandma 52
Flowers 53
Catastrophe Physics...55
When Was This? 56
Persistence 58
Jazz Haiku...59
Shame Circles 60
Fledgling...62
In the Milk-Calm Lake 63

IV   65

Breakthrough 66
Capital Punishment 67
The Tragedy of Love..69
Prayer..70
What Artist 71
Chipmunks..72
Raven 73
The View from Here 74
Heaven 75
Paper Cut 76
His Name Was Eugene 77
On Ignorant Design 78
The Same Old Questions...79
Entering the Stream (A Fractured Sonnet) 80
Evening on Karl Johan Street, 1892 81
Acknowledgements iii
Biography v

I

Tragedy in the Arugula Aisle

Want to have a little fun?
Walk into Whole Paycheck
(our name for a certain high-end
grocery chain) and ask one of those
food fanatics where they keep the
Diet Pepsi. Stand clear and watch
his head, and those of his colleagues,
explode. Watch those decapitated
food ninnies run full bore into the
granola and knock over the raw honey
display. Try to dodge the rivulets
of Apis excreta as it flows like
health food lava down the goat
cheese aisle into the kale, arugula,
and legume bins. Listen to one of
the organic food colonels chortle
about how deadly diet cola is, how
it removes rust from worn spoons
and forks, watch his eyes pop out
of their sockets when you explain
that's why you drink the stuff.
"No rusty parts in my innards!"
you say. Stay calm when
the Gluten Free Police throw you
and your reusable grocery bags out
of the store and onto your keister.
Want more fun? Stroll into the vegan
section and tell a stock boy how
great Spam tastes when slathered
with yellow mustard and nestled
between slices of Wonder Bread;
or stand in the middle of the coconut
water and oat milk aisle and loudly
complain that you can't find the
Sweet'N Low. There's much fun
to be had. The possibilities are endless.

Toads in Bermuda

Only one cashier at the Giant Eagle today.
      I'm stuck in aisle seven that begins
with broth, stock, and soup
      and ends with canned vegetables.

I stare at a can of Jolly Green Giant green beans
      and wonder if, at 72, I'll live long enough
to get to the beef broth, much less to Amber,
      the patient and weary checkout lady.

Everyone fiddles with their phones. I pull
      mine out and say to the young couple
behind me that I'm calling my attorney because
      I want to make out my will. They egg

me on with laughter. Let's gather kindling, I say,
      make a fire, roast s'mores, sing Kumbaya.
We're bonding, I say, and they laugh some more—
      laugh at the old coot in aisle seven near the veggies.

Earlier, at the deli, a sign reads, "Everyone's having
      trouble getting workers. Be kind to the ones
that showed up." A man behind the counter says,
      "Can I help you?" "Is that a Boston accent

I hear?" I ask. "Actually," he says, "I'm English.
      Been in Pittsburgh for forty years." I learn
that if you're from England and live in Pittsburgh for
      forty years, you sound like you're from Boston.

Later, in the grossly understaffed post office, where
      Janelle, the sweetest and most patient person
on the planet, is, as usual, the sole agent at the window,
      a man in line behind me asks where the Express

Mail envelopes are. "Is that an Australian accent I hear?"
    I ask. "No," he says, "I'm from Bermuda."
"We used to vacation there when our son was little,"
    I say. I tell him how Ari and I would go on

toad hunts at night, how the toads, of which there were
    hundreds, would exude an hallucinogenic spray
when you picked them up. Once, when my wife asked
    Ari how the toad hunt went, he said, "That un-
conscionable toad peed on my daddy," which was pretty
    sophisticated for a 5-year-old. In the morning
we'd find hundreds of toads flattened by mopeds the
    locals drove. "There are hardly any toads left,"

the man from Bermuda says. "They're going extinct
    along with bees, bats, and frogs." We stand
in silence for a few moments. Then he says, "We used
    to have a joke about the toads." "Tell me,"

I say. "Why does a toad in Bermuda cross the road?"
    "Why?" I ask.
"To find his flat mate," he says. We laugh about that.
    Janelle laughs too.

The Big Questions

Judy had to pee so badly her eyes
were watering. We had no time to take
an exit, find a gas station, and get back
on the highway to catch our plane in Seattle.

The road was behaving badly. Dust squalls
snaked across the freeway like snow squalls,
only brown. Traffic out of Seattle was bumper
to bumper, but we thought of nothing other

than Judy's throbbing bladder. Ten spasmatic
minutes later we pulled into the rental return
at Sea-Tac. A trembling man rushed to carry
our bags. "We just had a major earthquake,"

he shrieked. "Where's the bathroom?" Judy asked.
The man pointed a shaky finger toward the terminal.
Inside, the floors were covered with water and pieces
of Chihuly's glass sculptures. Police sloshed through

the muck with walkie-talkies while one man, wide-eyed,
mouth morphed into a Munch scream, walked up a down
escalator like a deranged gerbil. Judy launched herself
towards the Ladies' Room and found that the earthquake

gods had mostly spared Sea-Tac's bathroom plumbing.
And it came to pass that all the big questions—Why
is there something rather than nothing? What is the
nature of reality? How do we know what we know?

What is the meaning of life? and, most importantly,
What is the essence of relief?—were answered
in the less leaky, but infinitely soothing, sanctuary
of that lucky Ladies' Room in Sea-Tac.

St. Charles Borromeo

For Mary Holden

The nuns told us to pray
to our patron saints for special
treatment. There they were,
standing around in heaven
with little to do but check
lists of the living who had
their same first names
and hope that one of them
would ask for something,
anything to break the monotony.

>   Only first names counted—
>   there were no St. Jones,
>   St. Smiths, and certainly
>   no St. Rubensteins.

I'd pray to St. Charles Borromeo
from time to time, having no idea who
he was or what he stood for.

>   His last name reminded me of Borax,
>   the powdered soap Ronald Regan
>   pitched on TV and that occupied
>   most soap dispensers in the restrooms
>   of Cheyenne's many gas stations.

Maybe he was the patron saint of slaughtered bacteria.

>   Or perhaps he was a reformed womanizer—
>   a Romeo who converted and became
>   a dullard, hence, Bor(ing)Romeo, Borromeo!

Please, St. Charles, I prayed, stop my father from drinking,
my mother from screaming, and help me lose weight.

None of my prayers were answered.

Recently, I Googled St. Charles and was dismayed
to find that he viciously persecuted those who tried
to reform his church. Even more disturbing was
his portrait. He had to be the first to inspire the term
"you dick!" when applied to an obnoxious
or disgusting jerk. For St. Charles had a penis
for a nose, not just any penis, but one afflicted
with Peyronie's Disease. Yes, he had Peyronie's
Disease of the proboscis, which made him the patron
saint of both nasal sex and bathroom deodorizer.

> This rhino-revelation, this hermeneutic
> of the schnozzola, surpassed, for me,
> the discovery of the Dead Sea Scrolls
> and turned me back into a believer.

Laundry

Fat Auntie Ursal with her coffee breath,
baggy pink house dress, and worried
rosary beads would haul a basket of linen
to the backyard, pick clothespins out
of her mouth, and staple sheets to the line.

When it rained, I rushed to watch Auntie
panic-waddle into our backyard,
eyes wide, rosary flying, as she
pulled down the pristine sheets
as if lowering the mainsail
in a gale.

Later, she pled with Uncle Pete
to buy a dryer, but he couldn't hear her
over the sound he made while sucking
food bits out of the crevasses between his
teeth—a sound so constant and irritating
that it camouflaged his lifelong
devotion to penny-pinching.

Uncle Pete worked at Wallick and Volk Realty
in Cheyenne. Wallick and Volk sounded,
to my 4-year-old ears, like Walikenvolk—
one word. I became further confused
by my idea that Uncle Pete was, in secret,
a car salesman selling Volkswagens
for the Walikenvolkswagen company.

In those days, when Uncle and Aunt lived
in our basement, I was as clean and carefree
as those linens on the line, as innocent
as the wind that blew them dry in Wyoming,
and unworthy of all the rosaries
fat Auntie said for me.

Mother Wort

Two spices resided in my mother's kitchen:
salt and pepper. Her Irish pedigree prevented
       anything else. Let's pause to honor salt,
          something Marco Polo risked his life
to bring to the West—a spice that supplanted
refrigeration long before its invention.

I never knew about garlic until
marriage. Judy, my Jewish wife, put
       it in everything from leg of lamb
          to spaghetti sauce.
The entire house grinned when she made roast
    pork—garlic mingled with rosemary, thyme, parsley

and sage—a mélange to delight the proboscis
and incite lyrics from Paul Simon. Under my wife's
       watchful eye, my signature dish has become
          tuna salad made with mustard,
mayonnaise, onion, green olives,
and the secret ingredient—curry!

It's one of the few dishes I make that doesn't
resemble a ration provided by the Red Cross
       after a hurricane, flood, or house fire.
          My analyst claimed that
"We marry our mothers willy-nilly." Let
this man step into our kitchen while

Judy is roasting a chicken, or basting
a pot roast. Let him take a bite and imbibe
       the spicy fragrance of love.
          Let him admit his error.

Lunch with CNN

Ciabatta bread is holey, that's why I use it. Air is a great
weight-loss aid. I slather one slice with mayo, put
ham and cheddar on the other, cut an avocado in half,

then into four elongated sections, and place them atop
the ham and cheese. I smash the mayoed slice onto the
avocado half, grab a pickle, a Diet Pepsi, and I'm all set.

I turn on CNN, discover that AAA insurance will change
my life and give me more time with my kids, learn wire bras
are so last millennia, and that there are panties very large

women wear that are period proof, leak proof, even pee proof.
I bite into my sandwich and try to ignore the green mash that
oozes from my avocado. Putin's war against Ukraine rages,

and a devastating earthquake has hit Turkey, but there's hope
for men with Peyronie's Disease. Those crooked cucumbers
and bananas will one day be made straight! I grimly bite into

a pickle. Speaking of crooked dicks, George Santos has told
another whopper. This Catholic boy has claimed he was Jewish,
and that his grandmother died in the Holocaust. Does he suffer from

mild to moderate plaque psoriasis, or mild to moderate ulcerative
colitis, or Crohn's Disease? Maybe he lies to distract himself from
those maladies, or does he have Peyronie's Disease of the tongue?

Maybe he can't poop properly and needs the medicine on my screen
with its catchy jingle, "Number two should be easy to do." Speaking
of number two, I learn that Trump is railing against DeSantis for out-

polling him—two sides of the same coin, if you ask me, except that one may take a pill with a protein found in jellyfish that makes him smarter, because one is evil-smart, the other evil-stupid. Speaking of

overweight has-beens—Golo, Goli, Weight Watchers, Jenny Craig, and any number of lard-lessening programs await our Ex-Fraudster-in-Chief, if only he has time between indictments to try them. As for

me, I scrape my sandwich and pickle into the garbage. I've discovered a sure-fire diet plan: Lunch while watching CNN.

First Subway Ride, 1974

Surely, this is the acid test, I thought.
      First the leggy stutter down
the steps of the subway station. A man
      behind a glass booth talks into
a microphone. "What language is that?
      I ask my fiancée. "English," she says.

I can't understand a word.

We stand on the platform and wait for our train.
      Hollow-eyed men in torn sweaters roam
the platform. Women with baby carriages
      and groceries wait with us. The sound is
mind mauling. Our train arrives and, like
      lemmings to the cliff-edge, we push and
shove our way into the subway car. Graffiti sprawls
      everywhere—street person immortality.

The train screams at start-up, screams while the car
      rocks and rattles its way to our destination.
It must be about to uncouple, dislodge, break apart—
      send us into the abyss of the midnight
tunnels we travel through. Someone who speaks
      the same language as the man in the glass
booth announces our stops.

I can't understand a word.

We disembark. I check to see if I still have a sense
      of self, or any sense at all. I gaze back
at the graffiti covered train and smile. I, a yokel
      from Cheyenne, Wyoming, have passed
the subway test—got an A-. Now for the final exam:
      meeting my soon-to-be mother-in-law
who only grades on a pass/fail basis.

Dufusyokelsplat

Don't believe everything you read.
Socrates

In an effort to ingratiate yourself, you gush over
the checkout lady's name. *Mariam, so melodic,*
so original! In the midst of your obsequious display,
you drop the dozen eggs she's handed you and watch

the albumen, yolks and shattered shells ooze over
your shoes and coat the tile, so that every step you take
spreads the slippery splatter over the supermarket floor
and out into the parking lot. You watch Mariam's

expression morph from grudging tolerance to hateful
despair, a transformation that makes her question not only
why she needs this job, but why she was ever born. You
have committed a Dufusyokelsplat, so named after Colonel

Rufus William Dufusyokelsplat, a lost-to-history Confederate
commander during the American Civil War, who led a charge
against Yankee troops at Chickamauga in 1863 that would have
succeeded had his horse, Butch, not developed a severe case of

back-door-trots, thereby handing this important victory to his
boss, General Braxton Bragg. Disgraced by Butch who, the night
before the battle, nosed into the cook-tent and ate inordinate
amounts of baked beans, butter, and lard, Dufusyokelsplat finished

his days as an assistant embalmer for a Tennessee undertaker. You
ponder how Dufusyokelsplat became not even a footnote to history,
and you think about yourself who, a few years after your death,
no one will remember—as if you'd never been here, as if you'd

never held the one you love in close embrace, danced with her
against the throng, taught a young boy to swing a bat, or pitch
a tent, or, while desperate to impress someone you didn't know,
dropped a dozen eggs in a grocery store and made a mess.

My First Rodeo

It's the truth even if it didn't happen.
Ken Kesey

Janice reminded me of a dour, though
        pissed-off, coyote—the kind that would
        lope along the desert like a depressed
marsupial, then lunge at some unsuspecting
        vole and gobble it in one gulp.

Janice hated men, and, since I was unmistakably
        a man, she made our time together
        a living hell except, of course, in bed.
She was a wildcat in between the sheets,
        had the endurance of a Brahma Bull.

I rarely lasted past the regulation eight
        seconds before she bucked me off,
        but the five or six or seven seconds
were worth it. And just to illustrate, once
        again, that you can't tell a cow

by pulling its udder, Janice was deeply religious.
        She insisted that our bedroom frolics
        take place only on Friday nights. That
way she had to endure the threat of eternal
        damnation only until Saturday afternoon

confession. She was a fervent member of Saint
        Belinda the Bewildered's church on
        Carey Avenue in Cheyenne, but her
most devout devotion was to her patron saint,
        Saint Jan the Humiliated—martyred

in the third century A.D. in the most gruesome
        fashion. They immersed her in a primitive
        Roman version of a deep fryer when she
refused to concubine her captors. St. Jan's
        courage and convictions were admirable,

but when my Janice demanded that I loan her
        the money to start her St. Jan's Fried
        Chicken and Fish franchise, I took my
stallion, so to speak, and rode off into the sunset.

I'm Not Writing a Poem

I'm not writing a poem about smashing a wasp
that's bugging me on my back porch in Pittsburgh
with Rick Lupert's new poetry collection,
I'm Not Writing a Book of Poems in Hawaii.
To write such a poem would memorialize
and glorify a barbarous act that's totally
against the principles of my lackluster,
fallen away, pseudo-Buddhism—my feeling
that, at this age, I don't want to kill anything,

and yet, that's not entirely true. Gerry Spence,
the famous Wyoming attorney, asked a client
on the way to his execution, why he murdered
the man he killed. "Some people," he told Gerry,
"need killin'." And at this old age of mine,
I'm sorry to say, he's right. Some people
in our troubled world need killin', but not,
of course, by me. It's the same with the beef
I eat: someone else kills the bulls.

Ice Jam

And now, at 72, I wonder when my brain
        began its revolt in earnest.
Was it at a writers' retreat in the nineties
        when I saw my wife standing
with her back turned to me, talking
        to some fellow writers, and I
slipped behind her and squeezed her
        left butt cheek only to discover
how outraged a different woman with
        the same build could become? Or
was it just recently when I couldn't remember
        the name of the "prophet" everyone
swore by in the late sixties? No, it wasn't
        the guy who invented Scientology (what's
his name?), it wasn't Nostradamus—the fellow
        I couldn't remember died in the nineteen forties.
It certainly wasn't Ken Kesey, the name that invaded
        my consciousness and prohibited me
from conjuring any other name. (Why couldn't
        it be Ken Kesey? Maybe all that
electric Kool-Aid altered his neurons, enabled
        him to see into the future like the dude
whose name I couldn't remember.) I was so
        frustrated that I stomped my feet, but
couldn't Rumpelstiltskin the name into my psyche.
        It wasn't until hours later, in the middle
of detailing the recipe I use to make turkey soup—
        the gobbler's carcass, of course, immersed
in my huge white soup pot, with garlic, bay leaf,
        onion, carrots, celery, and the magic
ingredient, hot curry powder—that the name
        came to me—Edgar Cayce. Maybe
the word "magic" did it. I don't know. My
        wife and I call this process of remembering
breaking-up the ice jam—the name pops up
        out of nowhere and you get to return to
the illusion that you're not so old, that your
        mind is just fine, that everything will be OK.

17

Hypocrititis

Do you suffer from the need to have a twice-impeached, multi-indicted, adjudicated sex abuser do your thinking for you? Are family values critical to your identity and yet you blindly follow a man who brags about grabbing women's genitals and who had an affair with a porn star four months after his third wife gave birth to their son? Do you call yourself a Christian, then tell an 11-year-old rape victim that she must carry her baby to term? Do you chortle that you are pro-life but advocate for the death penalty and refuse to support childcare programs and school lunches for all those unwanted babies once they are grown? Are you more concerned about banning books children read about gays than banning the automatic weapons used to kill those children? Do you think that Neo-Nazi's chanting "Jews will not replace us" are "very fine people"? Do you rail against socialism then demand that the government keep its hands off your Medicare? You may be suffering from moderate to severe Hypocrititis! Ask your doctor about OxyMoron. Thirty infusions of OxyMoron delivered anally each month should help you regain some consistency and reason. (Rubber turkey baster delivery device sold separately.) Some people using OxyMoron have developed Musicus Flatulence Perpetuum, a bewildering disorder that causes the anus to hum, "I'm a Yankee Doodle Dandy," during sexual congress. Don't take OxyMoron if you are allergic to truth and facts as doing so may cause every mirror in your home to explode. Call your doctor and stop taking OxyMoron immediately if you begin to tell the truth compulsively when discretion would be best (a rare condition called Candorrhea). Your road back to consensual reality and critical thinking is waiting at the tip of your turkey baster. Ask your doctor about OxyMoron today!

Eraser Poem

Pink nub at the end of my pencil harbors mercy for my imperfect self,
the same self-taught by nuns
to imitate the perfection of Christ.

In first grade, we were given husky black pencils. No erasers.
Wasn't that pushing imitation toward transubstantiation?
Weren't they insisting we actually be perfect?

We'd use paste, our grimy fingers, crusts of bread
or tortilla parts to eradicate our glaring mistakes.
Our worksheets often resembled Swiss cheese, spavined
by the shattered windows of our egregious errors.

Our spiritual wardens erased the achievement
of Edward Nairne, English engineer who, in 1770, discovered
that rubber could remove pencil markings.

Too bad the Church of England looked askance at sainthood,
or we'd be thanking Saint Edward for his invention along
with Blessed Hymen Lipman who figured out, in 1839,
how to violate the writing stick's maidenhood
by attaching an eraser to its less potent end.

Our Sisters, virgin brides of Christ, were not impressed.

Still, we've progressed, glorified imperfection, created
erasure poems:

        elide

             ensure

casket

        basket

de Kooning   Rauschenberg

     death

          sex.

Dasein's Destiny

The physicists and engineers who invented the faux
modern boiler system with its labyrinthine tangle
of pipes and levers through which water radiates,
were not to blame; nor was the primitive urge of

primates to seek warmth, or the outlandish hubris of
Prometheus. It wasn't anything Dave did. Dave, our 400-
pound plumber, who, just the day before, suffered a
concussion when a drunk hit his car on his way to church.

Nor was it the fault of his assistant, Bryan, who shut off
two valves on our boiler on Friday because our whatsit tank
had a hole in it. Certainly, no one could blame my sweet
wife, who turned the temperature up to 71 when I wasn't

looking, causing me to awaken from a dream in which I
was intensely negotiating with Satan. Were the lawyers
and executives who dotted the "Js" and crossed the "Xs"
to blame, even though they excluded plumbing from the

homeowner's policy we'd paid thousands for over the years?
Strange to think that plumbing isn't part of a home (should
we have built an outhouse in our backyard?). No, as much
as these agents of penury should find their very existence

on the planet shameful, they weren't to blame. What about
God? Is They (to use modern parlance) at fault? If I believed,
I'd sue every church within a five-mile radius of my home.
As God's representatives on earth, those religions should

be responsible for His, Her, Their actions. But what court would
accept my suit? And if I won, which denomination would
ante-up? No, such a legal ploy would be the very definition
of frivolity. It seems that the water billowing from our blown

20

radiator, seeping into our hardwood floor, turning our laundry room into a temporary rain forest—this catastrophe is simply Dasein, down and dirty, being in the world, toward death— Dasein, who's fallen and can't get up.

Bring 'Em Young

Steve read the *Book of Mormon* to me until I wanted
to vaporize the Angel Moroni with a fire extinguisher.
(Would that work?) Those jokers in university housing
must have had a hoot pairing me, an avowed atheist,

with a devout member of the LDS church. Steve couldn't
drink alcohol or caffeine, or use tobacco, substances that
I abused with abandon. One morning, after too many rum
and Cokes, I burst into our room, turned on the lights,

and woke up my roomie. "A voice spoke to me out of the
heavens tonight," I bellowed. Steve, a big believer in miracles,
rubbed his eyes. "What did it say," he asked. I paused, and in
my most biblical baritone intoned, "It said, 'Don't bring 'em old;

bring 'em young!'" Some days later I caught Steve dripping
a few pathetic drops of rum extract (12% alcohol) into a bottle
of Coke—an apostasy to both his religion and the rule against
alcohol in the dorms. I immediately reported him to Mr. McCall,

our hideously tall dorm director. Steve's tiny bottle of rum extract
looked lonely in McCall's ginormous hand as he carried it out
of our room. He managed to keep a straight face while warning
Steve that he could be expelled for using alcohol in the dorm.

And then Lloyd Eaton, the football coach, threw the Black
players off the team. They wanted to protest the Mormon
prohibition against becoming priests in their church
by wearing black armbands in their upcoming game with

Brigham Young University. This temerity resulted in their
immediate expulsion. One of the ejected, Mel Hamilton,
a guard raised in Boys Town, and I became close friends. Mel
and his teammates made national news as the Black 14. Fifty

years later, Mel's son, Malik, arrived in Pittsburgh to attend
graduate school. My wife and I took him out to dinner. Malik,
married, with three kids, had become, wonder of wonders,
a Mormon! The church had long since lifted its ban on Blacks,

the ban his father had protested. I wondered aloud where Malik
was staying. His truck, it seemed, was his home. I sensed
the struggle, the tiny family back in Utah, the faltering
finances. We offered our house. He stayed with us for

three months. After Malik left, Mel called, "I owe you,"
he said. "You don't owe me anything," I told him, and
thought about my old roomie, Steve—his puny bottle
of rum extract, his *Book of Mormon*.

Blawnox

Thirteen winters past birth, our son answered my question,
What do you want for Christmas, with one word, Bongos.

And where could those bongos be purchased? "At Drum World
in Blawnox," the joy of my loins replied.

Was Blawnox some primitive bovine monster, a horrendous
flying cow, that could terrorize Tokyo like in those old Japanese
horror films? Not to worry. Ariel assured me that he knew
the exact location of Drum World and how to get to Blawnox.

A drummer myself, I'd studied the kick-beats of everyone from
Max Roach and Joe Morello to Ringo. This papa was proud that
his little drumstick had struck so close to his paternal snare drum.

I donned a skimpy jacket on that sunny, but cold, December day in Pittsburgh,
certain that my budding percussionist knew exactly where we were going. He
expertly got us to Blawnox—had me park two or three blocks from the store.

After five frosty blocks I asked if we were close. Only a block to go, he said.
Five blocks later I was pissed. I spied a business's door and said,
through chattering teeth, "Get in there and ask for directions!"

Ari entered the store and immediately walked out. I got so hot I could have
nuked him. "Get back in there and ask for directions," I bellowed. "Daaaad!"
Ari said, and pointed to the storefront window. Still simmering and shivering,
I looked. A mannequin stood in the window dressed in women's underwear.

Something was amiss. There were holes in the bra where a woman's nipples
belonged. I glanced at the sign on the storefront. *Exotica*, it read, *Attire
and Sex Toys for The Discriminating Adult.*

It's fascinating how fast shame can regulate body temperature. I smelled burnt
ego, blushed the color of humble, felt the fever of remorse. "I'm sorry," I said.
My drummer boy broke into ferocious guffaws. We laughed and shivered for
two more blocks, found Drum World, and bought a pair of bongos that
would have made a beatnik snap his fingers and say *cool*.

Assault and Battery

"Sweetheart," my darling wife said, "There's
a bat in our bedroom." She's finally gone batty,
I thought, awakened as I was out of a dead sleep,
but then, when I sat up in bed, a bat flew by.

A battalion of ideas blitzed through my head.
"What should we do?" I asked. "Call the police,"
the love of my life commanded. "And tell them what?
That we are being battered by a be-winged rodent?"

Two cops arrived and caught our version of Spike
from Buffy or Bela Lugosi with a collapsible
laundry basket. Three months later, our son Ariel,
airily approached me in our kitchen. "Dad,"

he said, "there's a bat in the dining room." Was he
bat-shit crazy? No. A bat the size of a cigarette package
had settled on our China cabinet for a snooze. "What
should I do?" I asked the joy of my loins. Adorned

in winter parka, baseball cap, Covid plastic face
visor, and oven mittens, Ari looked like a bewildered
beekeeper or a psychotic, middle-aged, batboy
for the Pirates. He gently placed the collapsible

laundry basket over the somnolent beast, peeled it
off our cabinet's wooden trim, and threw it and the
basket into our front yard. Most importantly, I held
the front door open for him—most importantly.

Despite this rousing success, I began to awaken
at night hearing a battery of noises: a bat flying,
a bat crawling, a bat perching, squeaking, chirping,
or whatever terrifying sounds they make. Since

it was too large to keep under my pillow, I placed the collapsible bat basket next to me in bed. I had become a basket case! I called an exterminator and agreed to spend thousands over the next few years

to batproof my home. A horrible decision that keeps me awake at nights now as much as bat worry did. The bats are batting a thousand while I, once as mighty as Casey, have, like him, struck out.

II

Standing Against Wyoming Wind[1]

In Cheyenne there were no thoughts, only wind,
a wind I stood against on a brutal February
in 1969. Hands grasping a Bible, fingers cold
as death, I walked to my draft board dressed
in a JC Penney suit so poorly tailored it
could have come from Khrushchev's closet.

Ashamed of my conscientious objection,
Mother wouldn't let me use her car.
Killing didn't bother her. She wanted
a snool, but she got me.

Wind blistered the prairie.
Hate blistered my country.

The head of my draft board instructed me
to wait in a utility closet. I sat atop a canister
of institutional disinfectant.

What is it like to end a world—end it with a bullet?
Who has that right?

Old men were sending us off to kill, to die.
One of them fell asleep during my hearing.
They hadn't read my ten-page argument
for not killing people—my plea for Spinoza's
pantheism, the physics of sanctity, of sanity.
Every life is holy, I told them.

Coward, a friend's father called me
(not to my face, of course).

---

[1] Title taken from, McDaniel, Rodger, *Profiles in Courage: Standing Against the Wyoming Wind*, WordsWorth Publishing, Cody, Wyoming, 2022.

The freezing wind swept me homeward—
my journey bleak as mouth-mist
in frigid gray air. They'd never grant
my objection. Had there ever been
a conscientious objector in Wyoming?

My future—a pallid hue of prison, exile, or both.
The wind in Cheyenne roared, but I heard only
the silence of hopelessness.

Two months after my disinfected declaration
at the draft board, their letter arrived. My hands
shook on that wind-withered day. Maybe if I
didn't open the letter, physics would back up,
time would stop.

They had granted my objection!

I felt a gentle spring breeze sweep over me.
The brown-grassed prairie turned
a bright shade of hope.

Rattle Bag

With thanks to Gerard Manley Hopkins, W.H. Auden,
Thomas Hardy, and Ernest Henley,

I am Margaret grieving,
        the one who thought
that love would last forever,
        who shot a foe I might
have helped to half a crown,
        the master of my fate,
a dappled thing,
        a brindled cow.

I am the *Rattle Bag*[2]—
        the plethora of poems
on my bathroom shelf
        that pulled me through
the infection and depression
        of the worst illness
I ever had.

I thought I'd surpass Freud,
        write 24 volumes of theory
(one more than Sigmund—
        if you don't count
the index).

I thought I'd pound kick-beats
        behind James Brown,
or the Four Tops, or Percy Sledge,
        or write the philosophy
tome that would make Heidegger
        blush and Sartre consider
suicide.

---

[2] Seamus Heaney & Ted Hughes (Eds.), *The Rattle Bag*, Farrar, Straus and Giroux: New York, 1982.

I thought two analyses
        and 35 years as a therapist
would carry me through life
        on a cloudy couch.
But it was words,
        lines built of words,
stanzas staunch on a scaffold
        of lines that saved me.

And today, in our backyard,
        I join a chorus
of House Wrens, Titmice,
        Chimney Sweeps,
Song Sparrows, Blue Jays,
        and a Downy Woodpecker
whistle my way into their lives
        until I become a bird,
ready, at 73, to fly away
        at a moment's notice.

Love Bumps

I

While Ginsberg was writing about blow
jobs and "the last gyzym of consciousness,"
I, at 7, was looking forward to my first
Holy Communion. I'm sure Allen
was more comfortable in his second-
hand shirt and khakis than I was
in my silly blue suit. He surely got
more transubstantiation from a blow job
than I did from the bland and boring
wafer that dissolved in my mouth.

II

There's nothing like the gush and spurt
of eighth-grade libidinal excretions spurred
on by Jane's newly erupted love bumps.
Among other parts, our necks were stiff
from straining to see beyond the wrinkles
of her white blouse as she drank a tiny
carton of milk, her prize for daily communion.

III

Body bags packed jumbo jets transporting
Vietnam fodder back to the states
for internment. At our high school dance,
Penny's shift clung close to her luscious
form, the full measure of which I was denied
by the one true apostolic faith. Those men
in their dark gowns defoliated my garden
of love as surely as Agent Orange decimated
the jungles and farms of Nam.

IV

My job was to serve with love the patients
on the medical ward at Denver General.
Conscientious objection brought me there—
a way to care for people I didn't know
rather than kill them. Soon I moved to
psychiatry where we all twisted and
contorted to see the cute intern from

Harvard try to make a shot on the pool
table in the day room. How her miniskirt
rode up over her hips as her stick caressed
the cue-ball. She communed with me
in the med room, surely a sin against
the Hippocratic Oath, and yet, a gateway
into the sacristy of love.

V

I married her 50 years ago on top of
a mountain in Gold Hill, Colorado
(Elevation 8,300 feet, Population, 210,
Total: 8, 510 as the sign reads on the way
into town). She replanted my garden
of love, gave me a wonderful son, and
put up with my temper and quirks
all these years.

VI

We often wonder which one will go first.
Which one will make our home into
a house. Which one of us will glimpse
the other in every arch and entryway,
every measure of music, every wall
and window. In what room will the other's
shade spread its shadow, transform the
single one's days into an eternal night?

Love

You can smell it in the folds of her hair
or maybe in the steamy aroma of a street pretzel
in New York City in the '80s.

It might turn up on a baseball field, echo along
with the crack of a bat, or drift through a Percy
Sledge melody or the largo theme of Dvorak's

New World Symphony. It might live in photos of people
dressed in summer colors to witness two *amores* join hands
50 years ago, or get kicked around

by a little boy's cleats on a soccer field only to appear,
again, in his grin when he graduates college. It may
hover over a hospital bed, survive the stifling

unhealthy heat there, grasp a hand gnarled by arthritis
and pain and, ephemeral and effervescent as it is, seep out
of a grave and haunt the hearts of those who are left.

All In a Dream

Last night I visited our cabin on Walloon again,
in a dream, of course. I sat in the living room
gazing at the lake. Water seeped over the dream floor
and I hoped the new owners would let me stay if I
cleaned it up for them, but I couldn't find a mop.
They'd moved the mop from where I always stored it
next to the water softener in the laundry room.

Why did they do that?

I miss the pileated woodpecker's sweep into our yard,
how he used his tail to grip the suet cage to have his meal.
We'd gazed in wonder at this feathered dinosaur who
trusted us, over the years, with his grandeur and glory.

I miss the walk up Townsend Road to Keeble. When
the wind blew across Keeble Road, across the plot of land
we knew as Thomas's Farm, it was if some god turned
the pages of a grassy tome that chronicled the dives
of red-tailed hawks and the fables of how sandhill
cranes earned their rusty hues and primitive cries.

I loved every weed and anthill that adorned the brown earth,
even the occasional dead bee amid tall grass. I found a wallet
in a culvert there once—no money or credit cards, only a photo
of a woman, a child, and a card from Alcoholics Anonymous.

Ice shelf

We were in Prince William Sound sailing
in an ice field when our guide suggested
we leave the safety of our sailboat and slip into sea kayaks.

It was the first time I saw Ariel scared. Our
young lion was 17 and, while his boat splashed into the icy
water, his face turned white as the glacier that towered over us.

I, too, trembled with cold and fear,
but found myself irresistibly drawn
to the gelid water and the stark beauty that surrounded us.

Judy eased herself into our two-seater and later
confessed that she didn't want to live if Ari and I died,
so she came along even though we knew that, should we capsize,

we'd have about a minute and a half before
hypothermia slurped Alaska's version of a people
popsicle. The glacier was calving. Every time a chunk

fell off into the water a thunderous roar cracked
the silence, forced us to turn our kayaks
into the waves and ride it out. Terrified and thrilled,

we rounded a frozen bend. There, on an ice shelf,
lounged a huge sea lion—must have weighed close to a ton. He
seemed as curious about us as we were of him, though he was calmer.

After we returned to the sailboat, I understood
how kind our pinniped pal had been not to
upend us when he dove beneath our kayak for his afternoon swim.

Kindness floats in this desolate place of white
and blue ice, a wildness that can be forgiving, or not,
but for us, that day, it surfaced a scaffold built of dreams.

Getting It Right

Outside,
  sunlight stipples the monk's hood

Inside,
  October afternoon
    Rachmaninoff's Third Piano Concerto

A young Van Cliburn
  giddy in Moscow

Mugsi the dog snoozes on the couch

Boodles the cat bathes in sun

Judy's sing-song voice announces lunch

Birch branches tap our skylights
  nudge us towards
    colder days

Lucky isn't the word
  for this glory

Blessed fits better.

The Hearty Roar of Autumn

I wonder when our dog Mugsi guessed that
the leaves she used to chase weren't alive. Wait,
I tell her, they're beings that require
breath to blow them across amber-colored

yards. The same breath that propels the winds of
life, prompts our lungs through their vibrant days.
The same wind that skitters leaves across boulevards
and prairies, makes them bow and sway—their duty

to gods, maybe angels, maybe not.
The same wind that intones the hearty roar
of autumn and that, along with loam and
leaf, carries the aroma of *lebenstod*,

the fragrance of the withered, the fallen—
of what no longer respires but inspires.

Let It Be

Avedis Zildjian made his first cymbal in 1618,
but I discovered Zildjian cymbals because
Ringo chose them to adorn his Ludwig Oyster
Pearl drum set with its Speed King bass drum pedal.
I bought that exact drum kit in 1966, paid

for it from proceeds earned while percussing
with our little garage band, The Rogues.
I can still smell the chrome polish when I
opened the boxes housing those surfaces
that let me survive my mother's rages and my
many broken hearts. Now those drums sit

in my music room across from my study in the
third-floor attic. Their *Hey Jude* days embedded
in my yesterdays. Those kick-beats live in my body,
twist and shout their way through my arms, legs,
and heart, but not on the drum set anymore. Too
many friends are tormented by tinnitus, something

that terrifies me because of all the music that treacherous
tone would destroy. A philodendron and Boston fern
bookend my drum kit now. Dead and curling leaves reside
on the snare drum and on the floor in front of the bass drum.
The picture is one of a fall, the fall of a life.

Last night, Frankie Curran, long dead, visited in a dream.
I asked him if he remembered the cadences we played
for the St. Mary's High School Marching Band. No,
he said, and looked startled. You taught them to me,
Frank, I said, and proceeded to play the first one
I'd learned on the stretched flesh of my sadness.

The fall of life wilts everything. I live now
in a marcescence, waiting for the wind
to unfurl the curl. And yet
the beat endures,
it goes on.

Immortality

You make sure to eat Grape-Nuts
every third or fourth morning,
cover those non-nut nuts with
blueberries because they have gobs
of Omegas and no Thetas, floss
every other night to inhibit heart
infections, use mouthwash several
times a day to ward off armies
of oral bacteria, walk the dog every
night for a mile, eat an orange daily,
take your Lipitor horse pill, your
Enalapril, Verapamil, Singulair, multi-
vitamin, Allegra, and carefully cut
your Metoprolol in half and take it
for your arrythmias, and you do
all this instead of church, instead
of fingering rosary beads and
telling yourself that somewhere
near our galaxy's big black hole
Jesus and Mary are floating
around without oxygen masks
or spacesuits, and it's in this way
that you avoid the anvil of disease,
the miasma of malaise, the numinosity
of pneumonia—in this way you make
sure never to die, you make sure
to live forever and ever. Amen.

The Fortress

Surround yourself with books,
a fortress of paper and bindings.
Turn the pages—
Madame Bovary, *Vanity Fair*,
even *The Fall of Giants* by Ken Follett.
Live in those gone worlds.
Avoid mortality's stealthy creep,
its footprint lodged in your nightscape.

Your pounding, angry, heart
wakes you up, tries to escape
the dungeon of your chest,
its arrhythmic declaration:
Everyone must die.
You are no exception.
There's never a right time.
Turn the page.

Last Words

The sociopathic originator of Gestalt Psychotherapy,
Fritz Perls, told a nurse,
        "Don't tell me what to do,"
and stopped breathing.

A friend told his wife,
        "I love you,"
three times and dropped dead in his garden,
leaving the geraniums unplanted.

Some are clearly rehearsed:
        "*Noli timere*" the great poet
Seamus Heaney texted his wife shortly
before he crossed Lethe.

Jim Harrison wrote the line,
        "Man shits his pants and trashed God's body,"
and slid off his chair,
pencil in hand.

"Have a great flight," a friend's mother
told her, but died before she landed.

My mother had no last words. Her brain stopped
working years before she died. She slipped out
of this veil of torn promises as quietly as a burglar
leaving through a midnight window.

You never know what your last words might be.
Should death grab you *in medias res* they could
be as mundane as,
        turn the channel
        it's cold in here
or
        I only eat the frosting.

Even on your death bed the reaper might move
too swiftly to leave you much thought.

       Help! might be a last utterance
or
       I'm falling through the sky.

Most likely, for me, if I have time
and the presence of mind,
I'll choke out something like,

       Now what?

Shadows on Our Bedroom Floor

Wisteria and oak leaves pulse
across our bedroom carpet
on this sun-glad Thursday
in Pittsburgh.

Who could possibly kill himself
after gazing at this inverse world?

Window panes divide this shadow-art
into impalpable portions, portraits
of natural motion.

The tragedies of existence
shrink up against this moment
of mad glory, this tiny
life preserver floating
on the quotidian sea.

No bullet, no noose, no plunge
into the abyss is necessary now,
only the presence of this
priceless bequest,
its lambent grace,
its lilting peace.

Grace

It was Grace who placed this plant
in my study. Grace who used to clean
our house, who knew everything
about cats, who would listen

to our problems with a wisdom
we didn't possess, with an ear
that blanketed our woes as if
they were children put to bed.

It's grace that sustains this plant, keeps
it in my study up against a window
that frames the neighbor's hemlock
and the occasional winter sunset.

This plant has, by now, grown a bark,
its sprawling branches anchor its weepy
leaves—weepy because I only water it
when it's about to die. This plant

is an obligation, a relative you have to
feed during a visit, a boring guest you
must entertain, must endure, or forfeit
what grace you've garnered, or grudged.

Stinky

I look past my laptop
at the foldout couch
in my third-floor study,
the couch where Stinky,
my little gray cat,
would relax when she
wasn't clinging to me
for hours while I wrote.
She would break her grip
periodically to gently place
her nose against my nose.

Stinky didn't always groom
herself. She had an odor,
but with her nose pressed
against mine, I smelled
the most treasured perfume.
It was on that pull-out couch,
the one I'm looking at now,
where my Stinky suddenly died.
I look at that couch, and my heart,
even years after her death,
hurls down an empty elevator
shaft in my chest.

The day after she died, a song
sparrow landed and lingered
on my study's windowsill.
No song flew from her beak
that day, but her watchful eye stared
straight into my soul. She was,
of course, Stinky in her bird disguise,
returned to ensure that I would be okay
in my lonely study without her, that
I would continue, alone, with only
the tiny holes her claws had made
in the backs of my shirts, hieroglyphics
she left to remind me of her heartfelt
grasp, her quiet, soothing breath.

III

Boiled Dinners

They could take half-a-day to prepare.
       Mother would cut up turnips, carrots,
onions, grab a slab of salt port and most
       of a roast beef, toss it into the big green
pot, fill it with water, turn on the burner,
       then go do something else.

The house smelled like a place where
       I belonged. Grandpa would arrive
from Omaha, after riding the rails on his
       White Pass (he was a fifty-year man
on the Union Pacific). He'd open a paper bag
       that contained tomatoes, green beans,
and hot peppers from his garden.

Mom put plastic dinner plates on top of the boiling
       pot to warm them and then dealt them
onto our table. My job was to frame them
       with silverware and napkins. You could
cut the beef with a fork and the vegetables
       would melt in your mouth. Salt and
pepper were used to excess until those of us with

daring palates slathered a chunk of beef with horseradish.
       The war on our tongues resembled the battle
between the Archangel Gabriel and Satan for Paradise.
       Between mouthfuls, the stories began:
Mother told of Mr. McGrath who lived next door
       when she was a child, and who, liquored-up,
shot his rifle into the air every New Year's Eve.

When Mom was ten, he managed to shoot himself
        in the foot. Mr. O'Neil, another neighbor,
brother to Monsignor O'Neil at their church,
        would go on a tear at the local watering
hole, whereupon Mrs. O'Neil locked him out
        of their house. "Locked out of me own
home," my mother used a brogue to imitate him.

Grandpa told stories of Custer, Kit Carson, and
        the notorious outlaw, Tom Horn, who was
hung in Cheyenne in 1903. Grandpa twisted his neck
        unnaturally, bulged his eyes, and dangled
his tongue off the side of his mouth. "It took him
        17 minutes to die," he said. Mother cringed while
my dad laughed, swigged his Budweiser, and flicked ash
        off his Kent cigarette with its Micronite filter.

I'd eat my meat, horseradish, and turnips.
        I'd listen.
This was peace.
        This was a place
where I belonged.

Dodgeball

We'd line up against the wall like the condemned
awaiting mass execution. Vince and Victor,

the two best athletes in the fourth grade, their
hair slicked with Brylcreem, combs in their back

pockets, skinny svelte bodies snug within their
corduroys and penny loafers, stood before us

like the Crusaders we read so much about, guys
like Charlemagne who loved his daughters so

much he wouldn't allow them to marry, who
was so beastly and bombastic that he inspired both

Napoleon and Hitler, but I'm getting ahead of myself.
Against the wall, the condemned of St. Mary's would beg,

"Pick me, Vince." "Pick me, Victor." But not me. I was
a rotund 8-year-old whose only skill was prayer

and that didn't take off the pounds, provide me with friends,
or improve my athletic abilities. I loved that I was always

picked last. I'd make sure to get ball-slammed immediately
so I could hide in a corner of the playground and dream about

the lovely winter storm that would be coming. Cheyenne got
them as early as September. I'd watch those huge snowflakes

land like feathers and transform the world into a crystalline
purity beyond dodge or ridicule. No two flakes were alike.

The Green Chair

It was my father's pleasure throne,
where he sat, ringed in smoke,
Bud in hand, laughed at Sid Caesar
and Red Skelton, watched the Yankees
play the Game of the Week, the Saturday

Night Fights, and Ed Sullivan on Sundays—
that living room chair where Bon Bon, our
little poodle, pressed against his chest, licked
his chin, and swooned in ecstasy, her eyes rolling
to the back of her head out of love.

Into that same overstuffed chair my mother, beset
by rage, pushed my drunken father, sotted after
nine o'clock as usual, and watched his eyes roll
into the back of his head then forward toward
his nose and cross.

"Ward! Ward!" she screamed, metamorphosed
from a shrieking hate-filled banshee fisting my
father's chest to the Catholic schoolgirl he married—
imbiber of communion and confession,
the conniver who yearned for heaven.

At 10, my sanctuary was in our basement,
the hi-fi, Dvorak's New World, the grassy
hills of his *Largo Theme*—notes that
danced across my worry and skittered
like leaves across a wind-worn prairie.

My mother called an ambulance. Later, she
forced me onto her bed, trapped me there, while
she swore to God she'd never hit my father again.
My stomach tightens at this memory, even now,
seventy-two years down the raucous road of life.

51

Grandma

I wish I would have remembered the lilac fragrance
that perfumed a room long after she left it, or the creak

of her leather purse as she rummaged through it, found
her wallet, and pulled out one of the ubiquitous twenties

she'd hand my mom or dad. I wish I would have recalled
her sitting in my father's green chair, tracing the figures

on her Braille watch, or how she always cried when
Lawrence Welk played a piece of Irish music.

I could have thought about those poodle-dog covers
she crocheted, while blind, that fit perfectly over

my father's empty whiskey bottles—he wouldn't allow
them on the full ones. But the memory that immediately

springs to mind when I think of her is how Grandma
drank a case of Falstaff beer every three days.

Blind as she was, she memorized the route from her living room
chair into the kitchen where the "cold ones" waited in the fridge.

She fingered her Braille watch nervously all morning until
12:01 p.m., because to drink a beer before then would mean

that she was an alcoholic.

Flowers

My favorites were tulips.

        You loved gladiolas.

I thought the cup-shape of tulips divine.

        You prized the vine arrangement
            that gave birth to gladiola blooms.

Red tulips were my darlings. I imagined them swimming
      in my diseased bloodstream where they fought
      the white cells that proliferated beyond control.

        You loved the hues that struggled like
            gladiators up the stems of those glads—
        fighters like you.

Your lips—the first thing I despised about you—
      the thick-shaped smacking sound
        they made while you berated me.
        You resembled a carp gasping
          on a wooden dock.

There was nothing about me that you could be glad about.
      For years I thought my first name was Shitass.
      By the time you figured out that I was
        a philosophy major, I'd switched
        to psychology.

You never understood why I didn't major in business
      so I could sell glassware, restaurant ranges,
        and pie tins like you.

Your mother who told you over and over
      how much she tried to abort you,
           what was her favorite flower—
           the cactus?

Once I could think for myself, you didn't like me.
      You preferred the inflorescence crawling
           up the stem of your favorite flower.

As for me—on that wind-driven, dusty day when
      the priest commended your ashes to the earth,
           and you could finally rest in peace,
           I placed a single red tulip on your grave.

Catastrophe Physics

Today was yesterday twenty-three years ago.
New Year's Eve 2000, the hysterics, broadcasters,
and conspiracy ninnies predicted a collapse
of the universe—a physics of catastrophe.

We ate pizza and drank fake wine at Gus's
house. He dropped a pepperoni on the floor.
"Three-second rule," I said. Gus smiled,
"In our family it's the thirty-minute rule."

He gleefully ate that errant morsel. His wife,
Dora, bookish and learned, fooled with
her knitting and told stories of Hemingway
on Walloon Lake. Mike, Gus's brother-in-law,

told us hair-raising stories of his time as
a quality control officer at Ford. He set up
a sting operation that caught an employee
stealing heavy equipment he used to build

his own automobile in a barn in Detroit.
Mike's wife, Hanna, carefully cut slices
of the most delicious peach pie I'd ever had
and passed them around for dessert.

The millennium was coming to an end. We
counted down to midnight. Sure enough,
the lights went out—all of Petoskey went
dark, but only for three or four seconds,

enough time to feel terror and then relief
when the lights returned. No doubt some
good-old-boys at the power station had
a little inebriated fun. We toasted the

New Year and laughed at the perfidious
predictors of doom. Twenty-three years
later, Gus, Mike, and Hanna are gone,
and gone is Dora's mind.

When Was This?

With Thanks to Bob Dylan

Eucalyptus laced with gasoline, the fragrance
of I-280 as I swooped into San Francisco—
the smell I forever associated with California,
the freeway, and freedom.

When was this?

Car radio blasting "American Woman,"
Guess Who's guitar chug purled through
every pore of my soul. I was looking
for Suzi, my American woman who messed

my mind in a good way. Suzi with her
tight body and wheat-colored hair. Suzi
who introduced me to Dylan. How we
laughed with Bob on his "115th Dream"—

so much better than wading through
all those names for sails in *Moby Dick*.
Bob threw the whole crew into jail
for carrying harpoons!

When was this?

I found Suzi in Santa Rosa. I gave her
my copy of *The Last Temptation of Christ*.
Kazantzakis's Jesus broke into an anxious
sweat when the crowd wanted to stone

Mary Magdalene to death. He loved her.
Panicked, he said the first thing that came
to mind—the thought brought from heaven
carried on a fierce bird's talons dug deep

into his skull—"Those of you without sin
cast the first stone." How blessed he felt
when she washed his feet with her hair,
every strand of which he adored.

Suzi's hair was just as comely. She had
nothing to sin about. Her father gave me
a glass of California rosé. I took a walk
with Suzi, then said goodbye. I headed

to Denver General Hospital where, as a
conscientious objector, I'd care for people
instead of kill them in Vietnam. I was lonely
there, felt chained to the skyway like the birds

in another Dylan song. I didn't know I'd meet
a woman in Denver who would help me shed my
shackles, an artist who had everything she needed,
who never looked back—love minus zero/no limit.

Persistence

That monkshood Judy planted
    still stands in late November,
        poisonous to eat,
but beautiful to look at.

It persists, spreads its purple cowls
    across our garden, blends
        with umber hydrangea leaves
watched over by our bare service berry bush,

but it's the persistence I want to emphasize:
    those purple blooms survive despite

freezing temperatures, our first snow,
    and the wall of water dumped on Pittsburgh
        by Hurricane Nicole—it persists like
Judy persists, seven months of recovery from nine hours

of surgery, arthritis—come rain or shine—
    radiating through her body. Yet
        there she is, every morning,
dressed as if painted by Renoir,

framed by her wheelchair,
    cooking her eggs,
        pouring her juice, and later,

writing poems that sing their lilting melodies
    into every corner of our home—poems that
        make me and even the floorboards smile.

Jazz Haiku

Fifty years ago
on a sofa I held her breast;
some enchanted evening.

At dawn my sweet wife
is in tremendous pain;
sweet embraceable you.

Billy Strayhorn drove
these rain-soaked Pittsburgh streets;
a daydream for me.

Like a dark lake her
black hair pooled on my pillow;
a love supreme.

For fifty years my
woman held me close in love;
night and day and night.

Pain medication
my chemical salvation;
you go to my head.

Autumn leaves skitter
along dusty, lonely, streets;
thunder before rain.

Our love so intense
we are alone together;
a noisy nightclub.

Even in high school
your silky voice made me cry;
my funny valentine.

Shame Circles

I got the idea to steal a book while standing in front of
my mother-in-law's bookcase.

My copy of *Darkness at Noon* was ragged and battered.
Although it was the same Signet Classic edition
of the book I had, hers looked new.

I never felt like an *I* around my mother-in-law.
My job was to please her daughter and, by extension,
my mother-in-law herself.

> She had so many secret standards that
> I discovered only after violating them.

When my wife, her daughter, was hospitalized
in New York and I stayed in my mother-in-law's apartment,
I learned that I wasn't to rise before she did—doing so
disturbed her sleep, and her sleep was not to be disturbed.

Then there was the exasperated sigh when, in a moment
of wild abandon, I removed my shoes in her living room. *Oh My God*
her scrunched nose, pursed lips, and slit-eyes wordlessly proclaimed.

How I crumpled the letter I had written thanking
her for some gift or other—the letter she returned to me
with little red shame-circles drawn around my misspellings
and grammatical errors. In her presence I couldn't

talk loudly at the dinner table, tell an off-color joke,
or eat an extra piece of cake since I was overweight
and might croak, re-dumping her daughter
back into her management and control.

So I stole my mother-in-law's copy of *Darkness at Noon* in order
to assert my individuality, autonomy—my very personhood!

And yet, as with many women of her age and bearing,
not much got past her. On her next visit to our home
in Pittsburgh she asked, apropos of nothing, *sans* segue,
if I had a copy of *Darkness at Noon* that she could borrow.

I said I did and crept up, like a snool, to my third-floor study
to retrieve the book. When I handed it to her, she frowned.
I'd given her my dilapidated copy with its torn cover
and frayed pages. It was the book *I* had given her,

my first-person edition, my singular copy!

Fledgling

Then to the elements be free fare thee well.
W. Shakespeare

I never knew I was that stupid. We'd
flown across country, from Pittsburgh
to Portland, to move Ariel, our son, into
his dorm room at Lewis and Clark College.

Turns out, everything I did or said was
the dumbest thing he'd ever seen or heard.
By mid-afternoon, this practicing psychoanalyst
wanted to ring his son's neck. I was seething.

My sweet wife, herself a psychiatrist, reminded me
of how anxious people often place in others their
most feared feelings. It was our son, she insisted,
who felt stupid and awkward as he started his new

life so far away from home. His only recourse was
to make me feel even less sure, less secure, than he.
She was, of course, correct. She could always sense his
inner life better than I. When he was little, she would

take one look at him and say, "he has to poop." "No,"
I'd counter, "how could you possibly tell?" Two minutes
later he'd be squirming, jumping up and down—body
language for BATHROOM NOW! My sweet wife's

analysis carried me through the day, while my simmering
choler helped me leave our only child to his new world.
I hadn't seen how protective was my anger until, driving
up Maple Avenue to our house, no longer his home, Satchmo

sang on the radio, "What a wonderful world." My eyes
overflowed—extinguished my angry conflagration.
When the smoke cleared, there throbbed my heart,
weary and worried, in my empty chest.

In the Milk-Calm Lake

Still, in the milk-calm lake, she chews purple-white
waterlilies, content, for the nonce, with her slow
crunch soundtrack of serenity.

Beside her in the silky soft water, her calf imitates the maternal munch.

A rhythm surfaces, a duet of tranquility serenades this placid bethel.

Under a lodgepole blanket in the Bighorns,
my son and I watch.

We want this quiet closeness of moose and youth.

We desire this grace amid the turmoil down below where
the world has no place to turn, no respite from war and deception,
malicious ambition, malignity, envy.

We gain this momentous moment beyond time. Our feet trundle
over the pine needle floor, heard, though ignored,
by the wild duo in the lake.

We are joined together, we two pairs, in this chorus of danger,
love, generativity, and generosity—this ephemeral event
of blue-sky animal delight

IV

Breakthrough

Breakthrough dances,
prances, pirouettes,
after cracking its chains,
after plodding through
bureaucratic spider-webs,
and corporate flypaper—
breakthrough breaks free
just before it's slated
for consumption.

Conspicuous anonymity eats us all.
Like a rock disguised as Zeus,
we must cause this massive Other
that uses its amorphous power
to make us into everyone else,
strips away our individuality—

we must cause that monster to vomit,
spew freedom and free thinkers
into blue-skyed dignity,
into that place where
we are only ourselves
and no one else.

Capital Punishment

You'd best avoid the voyage to the bottom of the sea.
Jim Harrison

It's a capital day to spend some capital.
We are the Titans! What claim does
Poseidon have on us? Most stay close
to the surface of life, but we are the adventurers,
drawn to the highest, the most remote,
the most expensive.

> We grieve, of course, for the uncapitalized
> capsized, those crowded immigrants
> in the Mediterranean, families fleeing
> oppression, who sought freedom, only
> to drown in Neptune's unforgiving depths.

We, we have lots of capital. Spending is our forte,
our birthright. Some might open hospital wards
for children with cancer, or finance food programs
for our hungry masses, but we buy adventure.

Some look at the sky, find friendly shapes
in cirrus clouds, track birds in flight, listen
to their songs, or linger over the beauty
of a sun-dappled forest floor.

Some are satisfied with a child's breath
blowing out candles, the robed procession
on a graduation stage, a melody molded by
Mahler—pleasures that are priceless and free.

Where is the adventure in that? We jump out
of airplanes, hike kill-zones of cragged peaks,
machete our way through jungles rife
with parasites and predators.

67

What of a woman's thigh at midnight,
or Warne Marsh's sax asking how high
is the moon, the sweet smell of earth and leaves
in fall, or snow-mist bracing frosty cheeks?

We swear nuptials to adrenalin, live only for the moment,
forget that the future, while not yet here, exists—forget
that its name is hope. We spend our capital on hubris,
suffer the punishment of Icarus, of all those who
go too high, too low, and leave so many behind.

The Tragedy of Love

After Confidences, by Auguste Renoir

They've found a shady spot on this
summer day. His hat tipped back
on his head, he reads the news
to his sweetheart. Her flowered
hat bouquets her silken hair
and rosy cheeks. She rests her
hands on his strong shoulders, her
long white dress a drapery of calm.
Her little dog pants next to her red shoes.

This moment of peace,
this segment of serenity,
this prelude to the tragedy of love.

Thirty years later, he has ladies in other
towns, none as important as she, he
assures her. She is as bored as Madame
Bovary. Her bodice has adorned many
dressing tables. Memories of other lovers
fill the flaccid spaces between them.

Hatred envelops them like a chrysalis of ordure.

When they hatch, they fly together
in crazed ogees, chasing one another,
each trying to wear the other out, each
caught in a spiraling aeronautics of doom.

Prayer

O Great Bewildered Buffalo,
creator of all we see and sense,
did we, your creatures, spook you
with our wars, our selfishness,
and cruelty—our tendency
to eat our young?

Did you trot away toward
the tall grass, eat your fill,
and wait for snow to purify
what we defiled? Did you
hide in the vast thicket
of time, find solace in silence,
absolution in the sticky
syrup of solitude?

We roam the prairies of perdition,
our tongues stuck on the salt licks
of destiny. We build scaffolds.
We await execution.

What Artist

What artist is it who
        gives us the fall,
whose brush is a brisk wind,
        whose canvass covers
all that is built, barren,
        and bountiful?

Who is it that composes
        the crunch of leaves
underfoot,
        or the soundtrack
of folioles falling to ground?

What chef combined leaf
        and loam in Gaya's
gurgling caldron to produce
        the aromas of autumn?
Zephyr? Zeus? The old
        bearded man
in the sky?

        Or

our simple sweet orb
        that hangs
in the Ether
        slowly spinning,
still sustaining us,
        despite our efforts
to despoil her?

Chipmunks

The chipmunks in my backyard can
empty three birdfeeders of sunflower
seeds in a day.

My feeders are squirrel-proof.
If one of those hungry buggers
pounces on the metal perches,
the outer casings descend
and cover the seed doors.

In my mind I hear "Cowboy Joe,"
the University of Wyoming's fight song—
the soundtrack of my victory over the squirrels.

The chippies wrap their tiny bodies round
the bases of my feeders, stick their heads
in the seed doors, and have their fill—a fill
that seems infinite.

How can such tiny critters eat so much and not explode?

On frosty mornings I stand, holding my seed bag,
and stare at the empty feeders while my inscape
plays the "Mozart Requiem," the soundtrack
of my defeat at the paws of those furry thieves
and their frenzied appetites.

My inscape flashes photos of black children
with bloated bellies and fly-covered faces,
immigrant kids on the border munching power
bars, too weak to laugh or play, and the skinny
toothless man on Penn and Braddock who limps
from car to car looking for change.

I hear "Comfort Ye" from Handel's "Messiah," the soundtrack
of compassion, of there but for the grace of whatever.

Everyone needs to eat, I think, and fill those feeders to their brims.

Raven

Consider the ravens: For they neither sow or reap, which neither have storehouse nor barn; and God feedeth them. Luke 12:24

Look at me—

my kind was here before the comet struck,
before lightning sparked
your kind into existence.

I have flown through time, found seeds
where there were none, carrion, berries
and ants where none grew or crawled.

Long after your time is through,
I'll glide along the trout-colored sky.
How dare you use me in your holy books.

It takes up to three years for me
to choose a mate. When I do,
it's forever. How many of your

holy men are faithful?

Do you think it's easy to be me?
In the winter I grow extra feathers
to stay warm. I have to fluff them

over my body to make a winter coat.

I must constantly jerk my head just
to taste some nuts so an owl or eagle
or one of your cats doesn't eat me.

Do you really think that God feeds me?
You fools. Put your Bibles down.
Spend a moment watching me.

You might learn something.

The View from Here

Boodles, his gray furry body nudging
my pen, blurring my words in feline love.

Mugsi on our porch, frozen in poodle
posture for pursuit, the wait for a squirrel

to leap onto our locusts, our oaks, our maples,
trapeze from branch to branch, tease in tyranny.

Monkshood abloom in November as if Van Goth dappled our garden in purple
and added hydrangea leaves, umber, larger than a man's ear.

Bereft of leaves and blooms, our service berry bush
watches, in silence, proffering perches for chickadees,

blue jays and redpolls who peruse our feeders
from its twigs, distance offering safety as usual.

The sun on this fall afternoon, lending its soft light
to blanket our yard in its milky sheen, makes me

think of how hard it will be to leave this airy sacristy, the marvel of a quiet
Tuesday afternoon, listening to Chet Baker, in Pittsburgh, on planet Earth.

Heaven

You won't know your mother
        or father,
your son, daughter,
        or spouse.
You won't know, or need
        to know,
your friends, all the dogs
        you loved,
every melody and note
        that romanced
your ears.

You won't care about
        the milky light
of fall in the pine forest,
        the deer
that white-tail its
        mysterious paths,
or the untrodden fields
        of winter.

Moments where you spooned
        your lover,
meals you shared,
        the aroma of love,
wine glasses clinked
        before a kiss
in your garden—
        none of it
will matter. None
        of it remembered,
because you'll be
        in His presence.

Sounds like hell to me.

Paper Cut

How did I get it? What page
of my notebook was the culprit?
Or was it the novel I read? Did Madame
Bovary cause this cut while I was engrossed
in her adulterous doings? Or was it Raskolnikov
waiting for his landlady with an axe that got me to
turn the page thoughtlessly? It wasn't Robert Jordan
in repose on that pine-needle floor. There was no page
to turn. The needles were sharper than any paper edge. His
trigger finger placed him on the cusp of forever and caused
a caesura that no stitch could repair. That tiny slit winces
at the vast array of pain life provides: a man's empty
chest while reading his wife's love letters to another
man; a woman's bewildered stare as the axe handle
shreds bone; that oily taste when lips caress a gun
barrel—the strident clang of those places where
the bell tolls loudly for us all.

His Name Was Eugene

He was going to die. He refused food
or medicine—everything but milk
in little cartons and the D5W the nurses
hung on his IV pole by his bed. He was 50
something; I was 19. I couldn't
understand his wish to die. *What's the matter
with you?* I asked/nagged while bringing him
his bedpan, changing out his urinal, or making
his bed—my hospital attendant duties. *Leave me
alone*, he growled, turned away, hid in the sheets.
He had to sign some kind of form. I can't
remember what. His signature, the sight of it,
sent shivers of the grave up my nervous system.
It was written in arabesque, each letter a brocade
of death. It could just as well have been sculpted
over the iron gate of a cemetery. After he died,
a nurse told me that his wife and children
had been killed in an auto crash.

Eugene had been the driver.

Eugene had been drunk.

On Ignorant Design

The mourning dove, unable to move, spread
into a feathered ball in the middle of the sidewalk—
the last option evolution bequeathed this injured
wingmaster with its haunting call. On this freezing

night in Pittsburgh, I steer Mugsi away from this
fluffy gray cushion, its beak golden in streetlight glow.
I don't want my dog to be its executioner, though
Thanatos has already spread his black wings, ready

to blanket this gorgeous creature in his grasp.
How can anyone believe in a supreme being?
This is the plan He/She/It had millennia to devise?
No one ever described nature as benevolent. I take

cold comfort in its cruelty, knowing that nothing
more brilliant than the Milky Way deemed it so.

The Same Old Questions

What happens after the shrapnel
cuts through the gray matter,
severs the thread of life,

or when the bacteria finally
hail victory, win the corporeal
war, or those cells that divide

faster than Formula Ones at
Monte Carlo crowd all
the health out of a body?

"We'll all see God, but
not with our eyes," wrote
Jim Harrison. What do our

not-eyes look like? Where
are they located? What about
the right hand of God? What's

Their left hand doing? Where
is it? How many hands does
God have? When will we settle

into the crimson lap of the Great
Grandfather pictured alongside
all those Gospel stories?

No one ever returns from Lethe
to leave an answer, and if the
end simply folds into nothingness,

sucks the blaze of existence into itself,
a black hole of Thanatos, no one will
have a mouth to say, *I told you so*.

Entering the Stream (A Fractured Sonnet)

Are there waves in the stream of consciousness?
        Do they proclaim
                what is obscure?
Or do they guard the obvious,
        make explicit the thrum
                of the big bang's hum?

Do their slippery fingers strum a guitar and sing
        of the queen's beatific buttocks,
                or against all advice
shock the reader with descriptions
        of her pet turkey's perversions? Do they
                coach restraint or inglorious intrusion?

Those waves in the stream hide what they know,
and guide consciousness from above and below.

Evening on Karl Johan Street, 1892

After the painting by Edvard Munch

We had such a good time.
We must have a good time.
We were supposed to enjoy ourselves.
We were told to enjoy ourselves,
and we did. Yes, we did.
We enjoyed ourselves because
we must enjoy ourselves.
Life is about happiness,
and we are happy.
We must be happy.
It is our duty.
Joy has brought us together.
We are together
marching toward bliss
because we must.

One man
alone
walks past us.
He is not happy.
He is not one of us.
He is going nowhere.
We shun him
because we must.

Acknowledgements

The author wishes to thank Elizabweth Solsburg for her editorial suggestions on earlier drafts of this book.

The BeZine: "Hypocrititis"
Bluepepper: "Love"
Cream Scene Carnival: "Grace," "Economy of Desolation," "Tragedy in the Arugula Aisle," "Boiled Dinners"
Ekphrastic Review, "Evening on Karl Johan Street, 1892"
Fresh Words Magazine: "Breakthrough," "Entering the Stream (A Fractured Sonnet)"
Impspired Magazine: "Lunch with CNN," "His Name Was Eugene," "Raven"
Jerry Jazz Musician: "Jazz Haiku"
Juste Literary: "Blawnox," "The Fortress"
The Lake: "Rattle Bag," "Capital Punishment"
Last Stanza: "Ice Jam," "Dufusyokelsplat"
Live Nude Poems: "Immortality"
The New Ulster: "Iceshelf," "When Was This?," "Love Bumps," "St. Charles Borromeo"
Night Picnic Press: "Catastrophe Physics," "First Subway Ride, 1974," "Paper Cut"
The Paterson Literary Review: "Mother Wart," "Stinky"
The Phoenix: "Erasure Poem"
The Piker Press: "On Ignorant Design," "The Hearty Roar of Autumn," "Standing Against Wyoming Wind," "Bring 'Em Young"
Poetica Review: "All in a Dream"
Poetry Super Highway: "I'm Not Writing a Poem"
The River: "Grandma"
Robot Butt: "Last Words," "Dasein's Destiny," "Getting it Right"
Rye Whiskey Review: "Assault and Battery"
SALT: "Prayer"
South Broadway Press: "Toads in Bermuda"

Spare Parts Literary Magazine: "Shadows on Our Bathroom Floor"

Stick Figure Poetry Quarterly: "The Tragedy of Love"

Streetlight Magazine: "Laundry"

The Unconventional Courier: "Green Chair," "Let it Be," "My First Rodeo," "The View from Here," "Persistence"

Wilderness House Literary Review: "The Same Old Questions," "The Big Questions"

Words & Whispers Literary Journal: "Dodgeball" included in their Featured Work Section.

Biography

Charlie Brice is a retired psychoanalyst living with his wife, the poet Judy Brice, in Pittsburgh, PA. Brice won the 2020 *Field Guide Poetry Magazine* Poetry Contest and placed third in the 2021 Allen Ginsberg Poetry Prize. His eighth full-length poetry collection is *Miracles That Keep Me Going* (WordTech Editions, 2023). His poetry has been nominated three times for the Best of Net Anthology and the Pushcart Prize and has appeared in *Atlanta Review, The Honest Ulsterman, Ibbetson Street, The Paterson Literary Review, Impspired Magazine, Salamander Ink Magazine, The MacGuffin*, and elsewhere.

Charles Brice is a poet of wit and weight, love and defiance. Beneath the jokes and banter is the shadow of family tragedy. His father's alcoholism and his mother's anger wounded him as a child, and humor is a way of lightening the burden of guilt while healing occurs through awareness of the random beauty of the world. In one poem "Love", the poet evokes both the steamy aroma of a street pretzel in New York City in the '80s as well as a little boy's cleats on a soccer field. Through the power of noticing, Brice finds both his subject and his voice. Kayaking in the far north, he writes *Kindness floats in this desolate place of white/and blue ice.*
—Michael Simms, author of *Strange Meadowlark*

With tightrope language, Brice soars across the countries of grief and humor in these poems with compassion and enough wit to bear the darkness of a coming mortality. His narratives weave through the pages of this collection like a wistful dream. At its heart, Brice's voice teems with life and leaps out at the reader. These poems proffer a voice of wisdom, laughter, sadness, tenderness and ultimately of hope, just as the closing poem, *Evening on Karl Johan Street,* 1892 proclaims: "We are together,/marching towards bliss/ because we must." *Tragedy in the Arugula Aisle* stands as a testament and a lush travelogue of a richly lived life.
—Robert Walicki, author of *Black Angels*

Here are some reasons I love *Tragedy in the Arugula Aisle*. First, because it's called *Tragedy in the Arugula Aisle*. And because in one poem he says, "There's nothing like the gush and spurt / of eighth-grade libidinal excretions…" And in another poem he says, "I found a wallet / in a culvert once—no money or credit cards, only a photo / of a woman, a child, and a card from Alcoholics Anonymous" (a tiny poem in itself!). And in another he says, "The fall of life wilts everything. I live now / in a marcescence, waiting for the wind / to unfurl the curl." I love it because when Brice's beloved cat, Stinky, dies, a sparrow lands on the windowsill of his study the next day: "She was, / of course, Stinky in her bird disguise, / returned to ensure that I would be okay / in my lonely study without her." In other words, I don't know any poet who can shift so quickly from the darkly serious to the wildly comic. Charlie Brice shows me things I didn't know the English language could do. Which is why I came to poetry in the first place.
—George Bilgere, author of *Cheap Motels of My Youth*

www.ingramcontent.com/pod-product-compliance
Lightning Source LLC
Chambersburg PA
CBHW071355090426
42738CB00012B/3128